COUNTING BACK
Voices of the Lakota & Pioneer Settlers

I took the cover photograph, "Ride to Wounded Knee," on December 28, 1990 as a few hundred mounted riders approached the original massacre site during the Wounded Knee Centennial. Cold weather and snow flurries dropped the wind chill to about -50 degrees below zero. The 1890 massacre had occurred during mild weather, followed by a blizzard in which many of the survivors froze to death. It was befitting for memorial riders, walkers, photographers and others during the commemoration to suffer a bit as a reminder of the much greater suffering and grief that had long ago preceded them.

—James Cook

COUNTING BACK

Voices of the Lakota and Pioneer Settlers

Sylvia Griffith Wheeler

Introduction by Conger Beasley, Jr.

BkMk PRESS

1992   University of Missouri-Kansas City

CREDITS:

Research based on The South Dakota Oral History Collection, University of
South Dakota, was funded in part by The South Dakota Committee on the
Humanities and The National Endowment for the Humanities. The
findings, and conclusions, do not necessarily represent the view of either
SOCH or NEH.

Poems in this collection have been published in *Prairie Schooner, Paint-
brush, Great River Review* and *MidAmerica.*

THE WITTER BYNNER FOUNDATION

Funding for *Counting Back* was generously provided by a grant from
The Witter Bynner Foundation for Poetry, Incorporated, without
which this book could not have been published.

Michael Annis, Art Direction & Design

LIBRARY OF CONGRESS
Library of Congress Cataloging-in-Publication Data

Wheeler, Sylvia Griffith.
  Counting back : voices of the Lakota & pioneer settlers poetry /
by Sylvia Griffith Wheeler,
with an introduction by Conger Beasley, Jr.
    p.   cm.
  Includes bibliographical references.
  ISBN 0-933532-85-7 : $12.95 cloth
  1. Indians of North America—Poetry. 2. Frontier and pioneer life—
    Poetry. I. Title
PS3573.H4347C6   1992
  811'.54 — dc20   91-37984
                                                        CIP

BkMk Press

Dan Jaffe, Director
Rae Furnish, Associate Editor

For Diane Weaver Wright, my friend.

COUNTING BACK

Introduction / *Conger Beasley, Jr.*   9
Author's Foreword   13

I

Fred Pearsall : White Owl   20
Walter LaCaine : Ghosts   22
Barney Old Coyote : Whistle Water Clan   24
Jonas Keeble : Tipi   25
Barney Old Coyote : Medicine Bundle   26
Paul Picotte : Buffalo   27
James Burnett : Sioux vs. Chippewa   28
John Cummins : Sun Dance   29
Barney Old Coyote : Naming   30
Before Looms   31
Cornelia Eller : Sioux Food   32
Paul Picotte : Struck-By-The-Ree   33
Missionaries   34

II

Philip Heminger : Along the Missouri   38
Dave Bucholz : We Had to Stay   39
Vic Bowman : Flies   41
Jesse Whalen : Jake Gooley   42
Lucy Swan : Stars   43
Orpha Haxby : '76   45
Orpha Haxby : Trespassers   46
Brother Red Owl : Iktomi   47
Eric Heidepriem : Gold   48
Mae Eastman : Grass   49
Roger Stops : Plenty Coups   50
George-Kills-In-Sight : Crazy Horse   53
Woman Who Waddles   54

III

Julius Albrecht : German   58
Paul Littleton : The Agency   59
Joseph Stepina : Dante   60
Mrs. River Johnson : A White Indian   62
Marie Anderson : Oxen   64
Anna Begeman : From the Hague   65
Edna Schenck : Sod House   66
Rachael Ashley : Little Short Tales   67
Knute Stone : Alone   68
Abraham Tieszien : Dutch Oven   69

Abraham Tieszien : Lost   69
Matilda Dorman : And That Was That   70
Jim Buryanek : Mules   72
Church Bells   73
Walter Miller : Wallowing   74
Dick Siler : Was a Nigger   75

IV

Thomas Hubbard : Blizzard   78
Selma Alvida Benson : Married   80
Pete Lemley : Deadwood   81
Dick Siler : Katydid   83
Jeanette Agrant : Yom Kippur   84
Vic Bowman : Off to School   85
Mrs. Pemberton and Mrs. Dietrich : Calamity   86
Buzz Gorham : Bogeda Bar   88
Martin-He-Does-It : Cain & Abel   89
Guy Goddard : Prairie Fire   91
Mert Buckley : Jingler   92
Ella Deloria : Learning English   93
Emma Huetner : About My Uncles   94
Charles Barkle : College   96
Pete Lemley : World's Fair   97
Mr. and Mrs. Bowman   98
Vine Deloria : Wanton Apathy   100
Jim Buryanek : I'll Say One Thing   101
Gale Small : Tea Party   102
Alfred Ziegler : Tribal Land   103
Mr. Evans : A Welcome Cup   104

V

Ghost Dance   108
Prayer of the Ghost Dance Priest   109
Sitting Bull   110
Robert Norman : Wounded Knee   111
Mert Buckley : Fort Yates   114
Billy Powell's Smile   115
W.H. Stoddard : Hurley Cemetery   116
Harold Lee : Counting Back   117
Walter LaCaine : The Heyoka   118

Historical Events :
    Dakota Territory, 1743-1890   120
Appendix : Guide to the South Dakota Oral History and
    American Indian Project Tapes :
    University of South Dakota   122
Selected Bibliography   124

Biographical Notes   126

> *Ah, put your white man aside.*
> *I tried it and Thunder tried it.*
> *We never did have our eyes turn blue.*
>
> —Wallace Eagle Shield: LAKOTA SIOUX

INTRODUCTION

In a land as empty as South Dakota the sound of the human voice can have a soothing effect. Amidst the knife-whip of the wind, the crash of thunderclouds, the screel of coyotes, that voice — plain and unpretentious — can be familiar and reassuring. It reminds us of our presence in a place where, as briefly as a century ago, there were few human beings. It provides a kind of echolating device whereby we can orient ourselves to a landscape whose features have helped mold the traits of our character and personality. No matter how modest, no human voice is totally disembodied. It resonates with associations — past, present, and future. In its rhythms and connotations it carries the weight of its own epical strength, the story of a people encapsulated in the sound of a solitary utterance.

The poems in this book represent an important exhumation of regional oral history. Sylvia Wheeler has painstakingly combed through a mass of previously recorded material to unearth and arrange a sequence of gems that offer new insight into the formative period of South Dakota history. The "voices" cover an era roughly from 1870 to the turn of the century, and they fall into two distinct categories: Native American and European immigrant.

The historical period they describe is full of violence and pain, involving the clash of alien cultures in a landscape which, despite its size and sweep, was still not big enough to tolerate the peculiarities of each. Something had to give. One culture had to radically adapt to the belligerent demands of the other. The tragic contraction of Native American culture under the impact of the European colossus gives many of these transcriptions a poignant edge. The predominant tone of the native renderings is elegaic and melancholy; the immigrant voices exhibit astonishment and consternation at a land whose physical majesty is more than matched by the difficulties of wresting a living from it.

The immigrants who settled the land in the name of progress and civilization hailed largely from Northern Europe. They were Swedes, Norwegians, Danes, and Germans. Mostly Protestant. Imbued with a compulsive work ethic. Dogged and tenacious in their devotion to the land. We catch some of their hardship in Sylvia Wheeler's selections. The elemental landscape demanded an unremitting labor that brooked no frills and few idiosyncracies:

> I went to school about nine months
> altogether in three years. Dad said,
> Someone's got to lead the mule.
> Someone's got to get in the hay.

Like the linear character of the land, the language is flat and declarative. This is what life is; this is what it takes to deal with it. No more, no less. The landscape did not encourage the use of euphuisms or flowery similes. Reality could overwhelm you in a variety of ways: weather, Indians, crop failure, grass fire. The immigrant experience possessed a solidity and meaning we can only marvel at today. Adapting to the land was a matter of survival, and survival was contingent upon a stubborn desire to endure.

In a land where the sky seems to bow past the horizon, weather is omnipresent. Winter tightens against the earth with the force of a screw. Droughts bake the soil to an unplowable crust and dry up major rivers like the Missouri enabling a man to walk across them without wetting his shoes. Grasshoppers fall from the sky in hordes. The immigrant response to these threats was to close ranks, unravel the barbwire, and section off the land into manageable parcels. To cut, plow, and quarter. To refashion the terrain in box-like figures so that — no matter how deep the snow might pile or how wide the soil might crack — the land would always maintain a marketable value.

For the original inhabitants it's not the land so much as the invaders who bring misery and ruin. The vagaries of weather are measured in mythological rather than economic terms. Though a bitter winter might drive the buffalo away, for the Teton Sioux it also had the effect of scourging the earth of evil spirits. Balance is everything in native life. For every phenomenon there is its opposite. The world is charged with the energy of conflicting forces, the effects of which must be absorbed within a flexible world view. Hence the importance of the circle in Native American thinking rather than the square or rectangle. With no abrupt angles in which negative energy can fester or positive energy stagnate and cloy, both charge and countercharge are cycled round and round a circumference that expands and contracts according to the pressures that build up inside it.

By the time white settlers began to move out onto the South Dakota plains in the 1870s, the Teton Sioux and their linguistic cousins the Dakotah had inhabited a stretch of territory from the piney woods in the east to the Black Hills in the west for at least a hundred years, maybe more. They had made their adjustments to the rigors of open space, and with the help of the horse and the white man's rifle they had learned to live with economy and comfort. They loved this harsh land, and with a ferocity unparalleled in the bloody chronicles of resistance, they fought to defend it — first in Minnesota in 1862 with the Santee Sioux uprising, and over the next 15 years in various battles on the plains.

The 1880s were a hard time for the Indians of South Dakota. Their religion was outlawed; they were forbidden to speak their own language; their children were compelled to attend the white man's schools. Herded onto reservations, the various branches of the Teton Sioux were bilked out of millions of acres belonging lawfully to them by the machinations of the federal government. The shattering finale to this saga took place along the banks of Wounded Knee Creek on December 29, 1890, when an estimated 300 Teton Sioux men, women, and children died in a hail of bullets from Seventh Cavalry troops. What died along with the victims was the last hope of native people that they could resurrect their traditional way of life through the vision of the Ghost Dance. The legacy of divisiveness left by the massacre continues to aggravate native and white relations to this day. The gap is deftly underscored in the callous, off-hand manner in which the narrator of the poem "Robert Norman: Wounded Knee" closes his account of that apocalyptic event:

> I never have gone back there since it happened.
> I should have gone back there and homesteaded.
> Had some darn nice land, as you know.

Not all the poems in Sylvia Wheeler's collection deal with tragedy and hardship. There are some funny moments on both sides, indicative of an irrepressible human tendency to make light of the diciest situations. "The Woman Who Waddles" tells the story of how George Armstrong Custer really died. Not by a warrior's bullet or arrow, but under the suffocating weight of an obese Cheyenne woman who lifted her skirts and settled her voluminous buttocks squarely onto the face of the wounded soldier. The story not only adds insult to injury in the best tradition of Indian humor, but it may also have served as a welcome antidote to Indian women weary of too much jive regarding the exploits of their heroic husbands in the Little Bighorn clash.

There's a lot to single out in this collection: portraits, testimonies, descriptions, vignettes. Ultimately, what comes through to the reader is a composite portrait of diverse people who define themselves in the context of a demanding landscape. Like the fragments of a mosaic, the poems cohere into an impressive depiction of the best and worst of a cross-section of humanity. What we come away with is a richer understanding of the qualities that are required to make us more than mere survivors of the era in which we live. In the 500th year since Columbus's landfall in the New World there's a lot of talk about reconciliation between natives and immigrants. Critical to this effort is a basic understanding of the history and feelings of each group: *Counting Back* contributes to that understanding; the voices that speak in its pages dramatize the common humanity that landscape reveals about enemies as well as friends.

— Conger Beasley, Jr.
Kansas City, Missouri, January 1992

12

FOREWORD

I "translated" many of these poems sitting beside the Missouri River (dammed to form Lewis and Clark Lake, Yankton, South Dakota), looking out on Nebraska's chalk-faced bluffs. Downriver, I can see the bluff called "Calumet" (*peace pipe*) where under an oak tree, August 30, 1804, a delegation of Yankton Sioux stepped out of their canoes to greet Lewis and Clark. Clark introduced the Lakota party in his *Journal* entry of that date as: This *Great Nation who the French has given the Nickname of Suouex, Call themselves Dar co tar,*

It is easy to slip back in time except in front of me the "river" no longer twists in currents, or smells of mud; it shimmers, a lake under the sun. And the Lakota Sioux who rides past on his mower would probably wave me on if I asked him what he could tell me of the early days. He would probably say, as other young Indians have said: *Don't ask me. Maybe one of those old time fellows can tell you something.* No more do I identify with the "pioneers" than he with the "Indians" even though my great-great grandfather homesteaded in Kansas, not that far away. I imagine neither of us fully belongs to either group; I have some Indian blood, and the man on the mower appears to have some white so the line back deviates, and, in the American way, we can only romantically decide which path to trace to which past.

Still, on quiet summer days like this, I sympathize with Crow Dog, friend of Harold Schunk, long-time superintendent of Rosebud Reservation, in his "yearning to live in the past."

> If I had a couple of states, and I built a high fence around
> them and the same situation existed in these two states,
> say North and South Dakota, that existed when Lewis and
> Clark came up the river, and I walked over to this big
> gate and said to Crow Dog: *Here is ten bred mares, here
> is ten geldings, here is two stallions of the finest type of*

horses that exist in this area, here are the makings of twenty tipis. Here is everything that existed when Lewis and Clark came up the river. The Indian is just like he was at that time. Now, I'm going to let you in, never to return to what you have today—why, if I'd stick that key in the lock to open the gate, Crow Dog would be running full speed a half a mile back down the road.

Does anyone alive know how the old Indian lived? Now, you take my father, born in 1878, he's an old timer, but he really doesn't know about the old buffalo days and he grew up in the country. When I first came into service here, I talked to many fellows who were in the Custer battle, and many fellows who were in the Wounded Knee affair. I would say that eighty years ago here on the Rosebud Reservation there was probably a dozen fellows, outside of the government employees, that could even talk English. This is really a short time ago, within the lifetime of my father. When he first went to school, he couldn't talk English. Now, Crow Dog, he's between two civilizations. No wonder he gets all mixed up.

Schunk's 1966 taped interview is now over 20 years old which makes it slightly more than one-hundred years since his father was an Indian boy in Dakota Territory. Historically, that's still a "really short time ago," but Crow Dog's oral history of the old days, whether fact or part fancy, helps stimulate interest in the Lakota culture.

Counting Back focuses on pre-frontier Dakota through territorial days to the federal government's final confrontation with the Sioux at Wounded Knee, 1890. The poems are derived from taped interviews in The South Dakota Oral History Collection. On early tapes (1950s) old pioneers and Indians recall, among others, Calamity Jane; Sitting Bull; Wild Bill; Struck-By-the-Ree, the Yankton baby Meriwether Lewis annointed a U.S. citizen by the Missouri River, August 30, 1804. Robert Norman, 7th Cavalry veteran of Wounded Knee, tells what his unit had for breakfast — hardtack — December 29, 1890; what his feet felt like marching into winter; what provoked the soldiers to shoot more than two-hundred Lakota men, women and children.

In the American Indian Tape Collection, Walter LaBatte, Sisseton-Wahpeton tribe, traces his family back to his French fur-trading forebear, Joseph Renville, born in the mid-1700s: "Many, many winters ago before the white man came, there was a trader from the far East...." Barney Old Coyote, Greasy Mouth Clan of Crow Indians, speaks of the silence practised between relatives to avoid "the old triangle suspicion in intertribal days." James Burnett, Chippewa of Pine Point, Minnesota, tells of the old grandmothers hushing the babies when the Sioux warriors were near.

I have included a few poems from the Crow Indians who once lived in the Dakotas as Hidatsa Sioux before moving to Montana in the 1700s; a poem from the Cheyenne, involved in the Little Bighorn battle; and a poem from the Chippewa, traditional enemies of the Sioux; all which give a better perspective to the dominant story of the Lakota Sioux.

Lakota stories often have a timelessness about them which may be the consequence of putting the Lakota dialect into English. In Lakota a situation, a fact, is established or yet to be completed; there is no past or future tense. Listen as Walter LaCaine, Hunkpapa Sioux, slides between tenses when describing ancestral burial customs: *And the old Indians, they save the finger bones in remembrance of their ones that die. They make breastplates from the finger bones. That's our people. That's what they did.* And isn't that the story all history tells — *our people; what they did?*

I assumed it would be difficult to make poems out of taped narratives, but actually, the "poem" leapt out of the longer story, probably because in oral history, voice reveals emotion. And though I modified by selecting, cutting, focusing, and sometimes combining, the "poetry" of the piece did differ in voice from the prose. Moved by emotion our voices tend towards poetic rhythms, towards concision and metaphor. For example, look at a transcript of Barney Old Coyote's interview where he talks of naming Crow children:

> You know we keep hearing that the first thing that the
> mother saw is what the child was named after. If that

15

were true every child would be named "Grandmother's Moccasin," or "Grandmother's Braid," or something because the grandmother is usually the midwife. The name became a mark of the child as well as an indication of the kind of life you wished for the child....

But as Old Coyote becomes emotionally involved in the story, he breaks into repetition, phrase, and unconcious rhyme:

You might go fasting up in the mountains like they used to do. You might have a vision, you might be blessed by a greater power. This is God given. You might go to sleep and see something in your dream ... This is God given too. You might believe in something and somebody might give you a medicine bundle and that bundle has good effects. This is God given too. We take a god given child and endow him with a god given name so that when the person leaves us as a mortal being he returns to the Gods and takes that name back to the Gods with him. We know we can't use the person anymore, and we can't use his name.

The poem I created from portions of this tape, *Naming*, became rhythmic by patterning the speaker's repetitive phrases. The poems reflect the speakers' conversational voices.

The shape of the tale, lyric or narrative, became the shape of the poem. Whites often recalled long narratives of gains and losses, ramblings sometimes disconnected, as disconnected as the pioneers from the new land. Indians saw their nomadic past before homesteaders came as lyrical, complete. Conversely, the farther away from the actual homesteading a white speaker was, the more lyrically romantic his perception of the experience might become. The Indian tale of reservation life often rambled.

Certain themes were repeated by both whites and Indians. Reservation agencies, schools, and churches gave Indians new names; an immigrant family name got lost in translation or was changed for social or political advantage. Interest in heroes' deaths persisted, though details varied. The old debate as to whether a "massacre" or a "battle" had taken place continued. Whites often repeated, "Times change;" Indians repeated, "It's a shame they (whites and Indians) didn't make their peace." Usage shifted from formal to less formal with each new generation. Words themselves change. Why, I wonder, did two old soldiers both use "squirmish" rather than "skirmish"? Did they feel "squirmish" about the battles recalled.

Counting Back is so named because the title poem reminds me of my Kansas grandparents' detailed counting back the exact cost of lumber and nails to build an early Jewell County schoolhouse. There is so much to count: the scope and price of land in their day as compared to earlier times; how many miles of railroad track were laid; what towns boomed; which became ghostly. The frontier was a particular place made of detailed particulars to be passed down, remembered. That the making of one people erased the makings of another is a sad frontier truth, a shame, a history.

These poems depend on South Dakota's 2000 tape Oral History and American Indian Collection, second largest such collection in the United States. The project was initiated by Dr. Joseph H. Cash and is directed by Dr. Herbert T. Hoover, University of South Dakota, both of whom helped and encouraged my research as did the South Dakota Council on the Humanities, affording me time to concentrate. Without the help and encouragement of Diane Weaver Wright, I would not have moved so happily along. And I'm grateful to David Evans who also read the poems and suggested the title, as I am to Dan Jaffe who continues to teach me. But, it is the speakers on the tapes who are the poets here.

— Sylvia Griffith Wheeler

I

They lived along the river where there was wood and water.
They lived along the Minisosa with the otter and beaver.
They lived along the Wakpawaste with the ducks and the geese.
They lived along the Hinhunwakpa with the fish and fur and fruit.
They lived along the Wakpa Sica which swelled and went dry.

Anonymous : DAKOTA SIOUX

FRED PEARSALL : WHITE OWL

—from a letter to his granddaughter, Harriet Blue, 1956.
Pearsall was an English emigre.

Your great-grandfather's name was Owakeyaduta.
Owakeyaduta was one of the old time people
who had been on the war path several times.
I used to have his old tomahawk head.
I never knew what bands of Wahpeton Dakota
he was from. But, of course, after the treaty
of 1851 all the bands were gathered
along the Minnesota River
on land reserved as a home for the tribe.

Your grandmother's tribal name was Tasinasusbecawin.
She was from the old Mdewakanton band
of eastern Minnesota. When she was a child
her family made a village at Rice Creek. Later,
they wandered all over Canada many years,
but some had the homing instinct too strong
and wanted to come back to their own country,
so along about 1867 several families came home.
Their only vehicle was tent poles tied
over the horse's back and dragging behind.
A frame was tied on the poles and a load
of blankets and kettles and things was tied on it.
They did not travel very far in the day
when the whole village was moving,
but young men on fiddle foot alone were swift.

20

Your mother's tribal name was Wakantiyominiwin,
a very nice name. It means *Spirit Walking
In The House.* Your mother was the only one
of eight children to survive. The birth
of a child was often an occasion of sorrow
rather than happiness. They would say:
*That child will not live very long.
Why should he come only for us to mourn.*

*My father had an old cabinet in his office;
inside on the smoothly planed pine boards
he could write important events.
I remember opening that door to:
FEBRUARY 7, 1887   ALBERT BORN   15 BELOW ZERO.*
—Albert Gushart: Spearfish, S.D.

WALTER LaCAINE : GHOSTS

They always did say there's ghosts
because somebody died.
They always did say their ghost
ate in the home.
And they always say: *Stay*
home three days after a death,
that ghost will be happy,
go away and never come back.

Somebody lose somebody in their family
they preach to them:
Don't leave your place.
You'll get stronger.
Be able to stand the grief.

But, just in case, they make a bundle
shaped like a person.
They put a lot of good stuff all in a tipi,
just for the ghost.
And all year they make stuff and bead
and prepare for that big feast.
They wear black and at the end of the year,
they cut their hair.
They don't cut it even, just cut it.
They put on different clothes
other people give them, and they use a sharp bone

and gash themselves all over.
They cut themselves on the cheek there.
They go barefoot so you know they're in mourning.
See, they got that ghost alone there in the tipi.
Well, in a year, they give a big feast
and they take that away.
They give everything away.

They bury their dead on scaffolds,
or in big crooks in a tree.
And the old Indians they don't touch
these things — the bones, the skull.
But some save finger bones
in rememberance of their ones that died.
They make breastplates from finger bones.

That's our people. That's what they did.

BARNEY OLD COYOTE :
WHISTLE WATER CLAN

*The close family of the Crow could not afford
the old triangle suspicion in intertribal days.*
— Barney Old Coyote:
GREASY MOUTH CROW CLAN

You didn't talk to your sisters.
You didn't talk openly with your cousins,
your clan brothers, the clan of your mother.
You could not talk to your mother-in-law
so there would be no suspicion.
You did not marry others of your clan;
they were like sister and brother.

If a member of a clan wanted one
of his own, he'd court her Crow fashion.
He'd wait for her down by the river.
When she came after water, he'd whistle
at her. If he was caught, he'd say,
The water's whistling.

JONAS KEEBLE : TIPI

*In my father's and mother's and grandfather's time
the Indian tipi was sacred. No children played in it.*

To complete a tipi, they would have 12
poles for some reason — 12 of anything.
And 4 is a sacred number. 12 is 4 x 3.
And pegs. Pegs circled the tipi and numbered
40. Well, everything's 40 in the Bible
too. Everything is 40. And the canvas
which held the tipi had 8 pins
and that means something, you see.
Then one door, and it always faced East.
And one rope holds the poles together
and comes down the center and is nailed
to the center to protect it from the storm,
to hold it to the ground.

Now, Grandfather said the rope came from above.

BARNEY OLD COYOTE : MEDICINE BUNDLE

This medicine bundle is a bird
handed down by the old chief
to his offspring. My grandfather came up to me and said:
Agiyese degagish.

"Agiyese" means one is watching over you.
"Degagish" is a bird.
The one watching over you is a bird,
a guardian bird.

It's a red power kind of thing —
now, I have some of it.

PAUL PICOTTE : BUFFALO

Old Grandma White Tallow down
here to Greenwood lived to be
a 100 years old. But you know
she didn't have hardly any gray hair.
She's the one that gave me all this —
she knew the Indian ways and all that
stuff. She gave me the history.

That hill over there was a lookout for buffalo.
No one private Indian could go out and kill a buffalo.
The old chief had his lieutenants and they'd locate
herds from lookout points, then go in units
to try to surround the buffalo and get them all.

Then they'd camp and set up some forked poles
and lay more poles across them. They'd cut up
all this meat in pieces — about that thick —
probably 8 to 10 feet long, and hang them over
these poles to dry. There were no flies, no potato bugs.
We didn't have flies until those white fellows come.

Anyway, those Indian people would take this cured meat
and go down to the river and cut this hay, the bottom grass;
it grows about 3 or 4 feet across, 5 to 6 feet deep.
And the Indian women would put the dirt in their dresses
and haul it over to the river where they'd dump it.

They'd put a layer of this straw down, then a layer
of dry meat until they filled it all up. Then
they'd kind of tamp that down and put some more hay
on top. And then they'd get this tops of grass there,

and blocks of dirt and place it just the way they took it out.

They'd go over there so far and blaze a tree
and the camp would move on to the next buffalo
hunting stop. In the meantime these lookout fellows
would locate more buffalo. So, when fall come
— the farthest away they'd get from this section
of the world here — they'd go back down river
to their cache, get wood and water to set up camp
and sleep right here on the ground.

JAMES BURNETT : SIOUX vs. CHIPPEWA

Our women carried knives and axes.
We had to protect our children.

You never heard a baby whine or cry
in the Chippewa wigwam. Like they knew
they had to keep quiet because the Sioux
were near and would kill them.
When a little child make a little noise,
the mothers, they say, *Cococoo,*
the owl will hear you, or they say,
Cicicii, the owl will hear you,
and this baby will quit making noise.
Always afraid, you know.

JOHN CUMMINS : SUN DANCE

I was told way back
thousand years ago
a man was sacrificed
to a forked tree
in order to live
in order to pray

You might say
you have a penance
you suffer
you get dry
you get hungry
you get tired
you get sleepy

BARNEY OLD COYOTE : NAMING

You might go fasting up in the mountains

This is God given
We take a God-given child and endow him with a God-given name

You might be blessed with a greater power

This is God-given
So when a person returns to the Gods he takes back that name

You might see something in your dreams

This is God-given
We can't use the person anymore and we can't use his name

Somebody might give you a medicine bundle

This is God-given, too.

BEFORE LOOMS

The white man learned
everything from the Indian.
      — Anonymous : CHEYENNE-EAGLE BUTTE TRIBE

The women did the loomwork on their laps.
They had needles, awls.
They made their own awls
with a little stick
and they made
a little hole in the center
and put a needle in there,
quite deep in there, and they use this
"Cha-she-she-la," it's like glue.
It grows wild and bubbles over into crystals
and they chew it until it's soft.
Then some animal bone glue.
They knew how to do everything.

31

CORNELIA ELLER : SIOUX FOOD

And the corn, a whole bunch
braided in husks, and beets and carrots
and pumpkins — all the vegetables buried
in a hillside dugout — wild rice, vegetables,
potatoes, everything. And it's full of sand,
and they bury this wild rice, vegetables, everything.
They put them in there and keep covering
up with sand. And spring comes and all the sudden,
somebody says, *Cherie, go down there and bring some carrots out.*

She'd take a basket and a stick and go dig in there.
She knew just where the potatoes and the carrots were.
They'd come out fresh and green. Airtight.
And then they'd make a fire in the ground with stones
in the bottom. They'd layer the food — first, the corn,
then beets, turnips, potatoes and meat. They put it all in,
cover it up for hours. Then, all at once, suppertime came.
They'd take out great platters and big wooden forks.
Everything smelled delicious!

PAUL PICOTTE : STRUCK-BY-THE-REE

Father DeSmet baptized him,
and he wore the medal until he died
— Paul Picotte

It was August, 1804, our Yankton people
told Lewis and Clark a baby'd been born
the night before. Lewis and Clark were camped
at Green Island on the Nebraska side.
Our people were camped across from them.

Lewis told them to come back the next day
and bring the baby. He would make a citizen
of him. So they brought the baby
and Lewis and Clark wrapped him in the U.S.
flag and handed him back to his mother.

And old Struck-By-The-Ree, Old Strike,
after he grew up to be a man,
he never did revolt. He got to be chief
of the nation. He made trips to Washington
and helped negotiate the 58 treaties.

I seen the old man when I was just a kid!

MISSIONARIES

*When the bell ring, they paint their faces red
and they go to church in their Sunday clothes.*
— Anonymous: HUNKPAPA SIOUX

The minister said, *Taku caje masteyalaka he?*
(What name do you like?)
He talk Indian to him,
so the grandfather said,
Jesus

And the priest said,
Nobody can have that name.
And another man wanted to be called Adam.
He didn't know how to say it,
so he said, *A-dom.*
So they named him that and baptized him.

But one day the old men went up on a hill
where they had Indian dances all the time
and one old man said to the other,
I shouldn't have done that;
I like to dance and now I have
to get rid of all my outfit.
And he started to cry.

34

He cried and the other one said,
*Well, we have to. We're baptized now
in the church and we have to live up
to it. So we might as well
throw away all our Indian customs
and Indian stuff and go to church.*

So they got rid of their outfits
and both of them came down the hill
crying, crying.

Oh, I could write a whole bible
if I had a little schooling.
Could write a history of myself.
Of course, we didn't think of it
as history in those days.

—Dave Bucholz : Wagner, South Dakota

II

Moon of the Birth of Calves
Moon of the Thunderstorms
Moon of the Ripe June Berries
Moon of Choke Berries Ripening
Moon of Calves Growing Black
Moon of the Yellow Leaves
Moon of Falling Leaves
Moon of Hairless Calves
Moon of Frost in The Tipi
Moon of Popping Trees
Moon of Sore Eyes
Moon when the Grain Comes Up
TETON SIOUX CALENDAR

PHILIP HEMINGER : ALONG THE MISSOURI

My grandmother who doesn't tell any lies
tells how she was taken from Fort Snelling
down the Mississippi by steamboat,
then up the Missouri from Davenport, Iowa.
Not only my grandmother but others.

And she tells how that boat
had to stay right in the middle
of the Missouri to avoid being shot at
by whites standing along the shore.
The Indians were shot at
all the way to Indian territory.
This is what they tell, you see.

And then the old people
and the younger children starved
to death on the way going up
so at night they would pull to some shore,
either side, and bury the dead and go on.
So there's Indians buried on either side
of the Missouri river up to Niobrara, Nebraska,
where they settled them.

DAVE BUCHOLZ : WE HAD TO STAY

Both grandfathers came from the old country
in the 1810s. They had tree claims
and houses made of mud.
Mud. Mud. Mud.
Wasn't a damn board above it.
If they wanted doors,
they had to cut them out with a knife:
no saws then. Man, oh man, oh man,
What an awful life! No one out here
but the squaws. You could smell them
for miles from the skunks they'd eat.
Never changed their clothes 'till they wore out.
Lived in those goddamned tepees —
how the hell they kept from freezing to death,
I don't know. No game whatever in the world,
just fowl. Nothing grew for the deer to eat.
What meat there was was salted so bad,
they had to soak the salt out first.
Then they smoked it too much. No
such town as Wagner then. No
roads, nothing whatever in the world
out here. We didn't even have a plow
to dig a hole in the ground. No
such thing as anyone digging a well.
No tall grass of any kind.
No such thing as hay.
No machinery to put up hay.
It's a wonder we lived through it, I tell you.

I tell you! Dad drove cattle out here on foot
from Tyndall. Man, oh man, oh man!
Just any kind a cattle, as long

as they had horns on them. Drove them day and night
until he got through the Indian reservation.
Most of them cattle died from the drought.
It was so dry you could walk the Missouri
and it wouldn't wet your shoe soles.
No such thing as a railroad here those days.

We moved out here from west of Tyndall.
1871. No covered wagons—
only thing I remember, Custer
used to travel with covered wagons.
No such thing as a house in those days—
call it a corn crib. It was built
of fence boards, just rough fence,
a double wall with dirt in between boards,
see, to keep the cold out when we could.
And we had nothing to burn whatever
in the world—I tell you, I tell you—
only what grass you could cut and wad
together and burn in the stove,
but in two, three minutes the stove would be cold
and you could go to bed that way.
I'd lay in that bed and sleep and look up
and see the stars when I was sleeping
and goddamned nearly froze to death laying there.
Jesus Christ, cold!

Later, when they laid those rails by hand,
10 or 12 men would get ahold of this rail
and plunk it ahead on the rough grade
then drive up the length of the rail
and plunk down another one.
No celebrations when the rails was in.
People were too goddamned tired to celebrate.

Oh, Jesus Christ, a penny was a gold piece
along side what money has got to today.
We aren't the land we homesteaded, I'll tell you.

What did we think of it?
Why, we didn't think anything of it.
It was here, we was here, and we had to stay.

VIC BOWMAN : FLIES

My dad stayed.

Before homesteading,
you could go to the North Pole
without seeing a fence.

All us breeds had cattle, horses,
big ranches. Then the homesteaders came
like a plague of flies and the breeds
moved out. Some who left were squaw men.
They went to Wyoming, Montana.
We stayed.

Homesteaders would get off the train
with a sack on their backs,
called it a "poke."
I remember old Billy Boy— had a horse
and himself pulling a wagon.
He was French and used to talk
to Granddad who could speak French.

JESSE WHALEN : JAKE GOOLEY

My father explained the prairie wind.

Jake Gooley's caved-in cave is a great big hole
Jake Gooley stuffs with hay till the whole thing's full.
When he gets a hankering for a windy day,
he sticks in his pitchfork and pulls out the hay.

So they came: Chief Waits Alone, Chief Four Bear,
Chief Charger, Chief No Horn, Chief Gall and White Swan,
And they said, "Some wasicu are asking for land."
And Chief White Swan got up and he told these people:

We cannot do that. We have children.
They have children who will have children.
Others will come. We can't give our land away
because our children and our great-great-
grandchildren will have none.
—George-Kills-In-Sight : BRULE SIOUX

LUCY SWAN : STARS

My mother said, "Never count the stars or you'll die."

Two girls were sitting outside a tipi
talking. It was moonlight.
Moon was shining over there, over here,
and they counted stars. One girl said,
That star going to be my boy-friend,
Well, that one's mine, the other said.

Next morning the first girl got up
and had a husband with her. She didn't know
where she was and was really lonely.
Her husband said, *I'm going hunting—*
you can visit your friend over there,
but if you're going to dig turnips,
don't dig that great big bunch.
They're wild.

So the girl went out to her friend
and her friend was married too.
She said to her, *You know, my husband*
told me we should go out and look for turnips.
Shall we try?
So they dug, but when they pulled
a bunch out, why there was a great
big hole. So they peeped in
and there was their own people down
there while they were up here.

And the girls cried down the hole

that they were in a different place
now with a different tribe.
Then they stopped crying
and thought what they were going to do.
One said, *Well, I tell you, when your husband*
comes back with some kind of animals,
you skin off the hide and save it.
I'll do it too and when we have enough,
we'll go down there and leave. O.K.?

One day they had a whole bunch of hides.
They stripped them, then put a stake
by the hole and tied a strip to it
and one girl tied herself to the other end
and jumped into the hole.
But she couldn't reach the ground
so she had the other girl cut the rope
with her knife and she fell.
When she got killed, why her baby boy
lay down by the hole. A grandma found
this baby boy near his dead mother, so she took him,
and she called him "Rock Boy"
and he always hunted and lived forever
in his grandmother's house.

ORPHA HAXBY : '76

It was '76. I was 9.
Going to the Black Hills
was all fun for me.
You could only make 12 to 15
miles a day with oxen, and Ft. Pierre
was the last white settlement.
We had to lay a week on the east side of the river
for the ice to freeze so to hold the wagons.

There were 15 to 20 in our group—
Mrs. Shaw's dray outfit, she owned the wagons,
and others, like my father, who were independent.
They just fell in with her train.

We crossed the ice and rode in the back
of the wagon until our feet got cold,
then we got out and walked until our feet
got warm. We had a tent and a stove
and were very comfortable camping at night.

My father was an adventurer.
He wanted to be on the frontier.
We didn't see an Indian along the way.
We were the trespassers.

ORPHA HAXBY : TRESPASSERS

We're dying off, you know.

When they discovered gold in the Hills,
Dad quit the farm and came up here.
No man ever went anywhere alone.
They always went in pairs — the dangers.

There were a couple of men who rode
down east of town just a little ways,
to mow some grass for their horses.
First thing you know the Indians
were trying to cut them off from town,
get in between them. But the commotion
was heard and all the men came out
with their guns and stood the Indians off.

I saw this Mrs. Johnson —
her husband was one of these men
they were trying to cut off from town —
well, they must have had a family row that morning
I saw her ball up her fists, then say:
I hope to God they kill him.
I hope to God they kill him.

BROTHER RED OWL : IKTOMI

The missionary is like Iktomi*
always spinning his web across the prairie.
One day he was wearing a beautiful new coat.
When he saw the buffalo, he said,
Buffalo, will you give me a ride?

Yes, the buffalo said.
But pretty soon Iktomi fell off
into this buffalo dung and ruined his coat.
So he went to a big rock and said,
My cousin, I give you my coat.
I love this coat, but am going to give it
to you because it's dirty now.

In the evening it started to rain
and Iktomi took shelter.
As he grew colder he thought,
Well, this rain is going to wash
that coat. I've given it away,
but now I think I'll go after it.

So he did and it was nice and clean
and Iktomi put it on and went back
to the shelter. He lay there, warm
in his coat, then a buffalo came after him
and rolled right on top of him and
that was the end of the beautiful new coat.

Lakota trickster *who plays on negative human emotions*
to cause trouble between man and nature.

ERIC HEIDEPRIEM : GOLD

Horatio Ross was a short, heavy set, grizzled man
with a black beard, mustache, and sideburns;
practically his whole face was covered with hair.
He had beady eyes — he could take his place
in any barroom brawl, but he was kind to us kids.
It was Ross, and McKay, another miner,
who discovered gold with the Custer expedition.
When the pressmen come to town to ask him
to point out where he'd discovered gold,
Ross'd hire a horse and buggy and take them out
3 miles from Custer on Crest St.
It was expensive and took time.
So one day, when a group arrived,
he took them down to the south end of 7th St.
near the railroad and said:
Here's where I discovered gold.

So that began the controversy.
They had a picture of Ross
standing there with his gold pan
to prove the spot. This made it convenient
for the Chamber of Commerce to include the 7th St.
spot in their "Historic Custer" tour.
Otherwise they'd have to lead people
out 3 miles beyond Custer.
And they might leave town and not come back!

MAE EASTMAN : GRASS

Indians go to the store;
they say, *You give me some food
and I'll pay you when the government
gives us some money.*

But the white man say, *No,
I can't give you any food
because we can't tell when
the government's gonna issue money.
So you go home and eat grass.*

Indians, they go home
to their village and they talk
about it and a few braves go back
there and drag the man outside.

And when the body is found
there is grass sticking out of his mouth.

ROGER STOPS : PLENTY COUPS

I was looking at the North Star.
The North Star is a sacred thing
because it never moves,
and Chief Plenty Coups came to me.

Plenty Coups had his head turned East.
I was facing North. He said:
See that eagle fly?
That eagle is my father.

This eagle was so old. It was black,
and some of its tail feathers were gone.
Then I saw an airplane
flying east where the eagle flew.

And Plenty Coups said,
See, the white man tries to fly,
but they die trying.

The white man, crazy as he is,
tries to bring me to his little church
when the whole wide world's my church.
He writes his own destiny.

He uses a pencil and he writes
everything down and confines himself.
He's a prisoner of his own laws.
Whatever he's heard he's written down.

And then he doesn't keep his promises.

*That portion of Dakota occupied by the various bands
of Sioux belongs not to them, but to the representatives
of an advancing civilization. The romance of the Indian
right to hereditary possession of all or portion of the
domain over which the United States now claims jurisdiction
is the veriest bosh. A power beyond that which takes
to itself the right to make and unmake treaties
between men long ago decreed that the American continent
should be given over to the progress of enlightenment
and the temporal advancement of those who are willing
to make use of God's best gifts while they are on earth.*
        —Yankton Daily Press and Dakotan, June 5, 1875

> *My father, Dog With Horns, said the Sioux people hated Lincoln. He said Lincoln could not contain his own people, why did he think he could contain us.*
> —Anonymous : LAKOTA SIOUX

> *Friend, whoever runs away shall not be admitted to The Strong Hearts.*
> —Song of The Lakota Strong Heart Society

> *We were not a conquered nation.*
> *Our kill rate was five to one.*
> *How could anybody go and lie on a treaty.*
> —Ed McGaa : OGLALA SIOUX

GEORGE-KILLS-IN-SIGHT : CRAZY HORSE

The one who knowed, Crazy Horse,
he stood by his horse
and sang the song.

He reached down
and pulled up one of them sand grass.
He put it on his hair.

He had a gopher hole,
that loose dirt. From the nose to the horse's tail,
he put dirt on.

Then he got on his horse and said,
Now, you watch me.
Don't go until I come back.

He rode right up
front of Custer's cavalry—
all dismounted and ready to fire.

Right up front he galloped,
singing his medicine song.
They fired, but he rode on.

When he come back,
he showed the black bullet marks.
They didn't go through.

WOMAN WHO WADDLES

Custer could have made a good treaty
with the Indians, but he tried to be
a hero, a togasila; he wanted to be
a president, and he tried to make some showing,
but it didn't work out. It would have been
a wonderful thing if they'd made their peace.
— George-Kills-In-Sight : BRULE SIOUX

There was a young Cheyenne mother running
with a small baby tugging at her breast
and Longhair, Custer, slashed off her breast
with his own sword, knocked her down, trampled
killed her. The baby died then or of exposure.
The Washita battle was in late November.

Beaver Not Afraid, this Indian woman's mother,
hid in a cliff cranny and saw all this,
and she hated Custer.

When Sitting Bull took care of Custer
a few years later, the Indian women
found him lying on the battle field
still conscious. They wanted to send
Custer to the Happy Hunting Ground
in the most embarrassing manner.
The Indians did not scalp Custer.
They hated him. They wouldn't touch him
with a ten foot pole.
So they got Beaver Not Afraid and asked her
to choose how Custer should die.

Now, she walked over to Custer, looked down
and said, *Well, go get the fat one,*
The Woman Who Waddles Like A Bear.
This woman was so fat she could not ride a horse,
and was carried from camp to camp on a travois.

So The Woman Who Waddles Like A Bear
got off her travois to look at Custer
a few minutes. Then she turned around,
pulled her big skirts up and plunked
her big bare backside down on Custer's
face and smothered him.

In one of the books on the battle,
Lt. Bradley said that Custer had died
a hero's death, and had gone to glory
with such a pleased expression on his face.

We must act with vindictive
earnestness against the Sioux,
even to their extermination,
men, women, and children. Nothing
less will reach the roots of the case.
—George A. Custer

III

Thunder Wheel

He Dog

Red Star

Spotted Wood

Iron Bull

Little Dog

Two Feather

Goodbird

White Weasel

Broken Leg

Once Sitter

Yellowhead

Spotted Tail

Three Legs

Different Horse

Thunder Shield

Rainwater

Chasing Hawk

Circle Bear

Holy Rock

Ft. Benton, Ft. Buford, Ft. Pierre
Ft. Randall, Ft. Yates, Ft. Sully,
and all that muster.

Abe Lincoln, Wild Bill, Andrew Johnson,
John Jacob Astor, Ulysses S. Grant,
and General Custer.

JULIUS ALBRECHT : GERMAN

And the teacher told me:
You'll have to stay in for talking German.
He was Norwegian. I was ten —
old enough to know better
than the teacher.

I wouldn't have locked kids up for that.

PAUL LITTLETON : THE AGENCY

They call him Cook.
At that time they didn't baptize,
so you had your own Indian name —
you didn't go by your father's.
His father's name was Black War Bonnet.
Cook was his white name.

Then the agency give him the name
Little Skunk, so when I went to school,
they said, *Oh, just call him Little Skunk.*
That's our name in the Eagle Butte office.

JOSEPH STEPINA : DANTE

Just woke up one day, 1872, said
I would like to go someplace.
I didn't run away from home,
anything like that.

Some guys talk about South Dakota
and I decide to come. Accident.
Something new. Well, different
people, different country.
That's all I can say.

I have to go to school here, Bohemian
school, to learn the language.
I studied carpentry.
I was interested in Indians.
Got a lot of friends among the Indians.

Was all Indian reservation when I came.
Later called it "Dante"—
they said it was "hell of a town."
You know who Dante is, don't you?

They were honest Indians when I came here.
If you lost your horse whip, they located
it and put it up where you could see it.

You know, they gave the Indians a contract
to keep the Black Hills, then they found gold

there and broke the contract.
Indians, they didn't cry much,
but they did cry.

Government told them to farm, you know.
They built them farm houses, barns, everything.
Indians are very funny people;
they don't like to stay put.

You build them a house and everything
and in a few months you go by
and see a tent in the yard
and in the front room two saddles —
what are you going to do?

They like to move —
they gonna eat with someone
and when they finish up that party,
they go with another family.
But all the Indians were pretty good —
pretty good.

People were friendly then.
Now, everyone's hunting money.
"Money, money, money. I need money."
You talk to some guy having a glass of beer
and he's gotta have it. Gotta have money.
Sometimes I think I don't want to die here.

MRS. RIVER JOHNSON : A WHITE INDIAN

When Pa died, the preacher said,
Here lies the remains of a white Indian.
Pa's word was law.
That's the way it was with all those old Indians,
Edgar Firethunder, Howard Badwoman, Tom Black-Eye,
Longskunk, all those Indians who lived along Bear Creek.
Honest as they made them.
But after the county was throwed open
everyone went to the dogs, stole horses,
stole hay out of the barns.

Ma stood up in that Widow's Walk and sang out:
"Here comes Pa! Up the river!"

> *It's the Yellowstone!*
>
> *The Nelly Peck!*
>
> *The Josephine!*
>
> *The Benson!*
>
> *The Grant Marse!*
>
> *The Far West!*
>
> —Pauline Kolberg : Yankton, S.D.

MARIE ANDERSON : OXEN

Grandpa Mellegard walked 40 miles
from Spring Valley to Vermillion
carrying groceries on his back.
Winters, though, he'd use the stone boat,
pulled by an ox. The boat had a couple
of small logs for runners and boards
nailed across like a crude, heavy sled.

Oxen could support themselves.
Horses were scarce, expensive to keep,
likely to be stolen. But Grandpa hated oxen —
they wouldn't mind and stopped to eat
or wandered side to side. Many times
he'd work all day, tears of sheer
frustration running down his cheeks.

ANNA BEGEMAN : FROM THE HAGUE

Uncle helped us pack.
Each child had his little satchel
of small items, linen and clothes, to care for.

The first two days on the ocean were rough,
then so smooth and blue. The meals were good.
We had a table to ourselves.

When we got off the train in Monroe,
I said, *Where's the town?* All we could see
were board sidewalks and little houses.

Mother lost her beautiful hair worrying
about this awful bare country.
She'd rock and cry, *This scheimig* America.*

scheimig: "dirty"

EDNA SCHENCK : SOD HOUSE

There are three layers of sod, you see.
They put down one layer, then the window,
I guess. Then another layer of sod.

Father went to Spirit Lake, got some kind of plaster.
They plastered that sod on the inside
so it wasn't sod. Mother whitewashed it.

We burned cow chips — they burnt good, you know.
We twisted hay and stacked it up around
the walls, and it didn't take up so much room.

We burned kerosene for lamps, but sometimes
Pa wouldn't get to town and we'd run out.
Ma'd take a potato, then scoop out the inside
and cut off the end so it could sit
on the table, then she'd put the lard
in with a wick.

RACHAEL ASHLEY : LITTLE SHORT TALES

When it was windy and snowy and cold,
we blew out the lamps right after supper
and got ready for bed. Mother would hold me
in her lap and stroke my hair and tell
little tales — little short tales about what
the Indians told their children and what
her mother and father and all the grand-
mothers and grandfathers had told before.

The wind would blow around the house howling
and sometimes stopping to make a little noise.
Mother said: *The North Wind comes to announce
the winter months.* And the Indians, when they heard that,
would make their camps and stay till spring.
The old North Wind telling them what to do.

KNUTE STONE : ALONE

I came all alone from Kolbach,
Sweden, 1878. I was 25
years old. I'd worked in a steel
mill since I was eleven to make
enough iron to buy a ticket.

I come by train car to Salem.
I had $200.00 in my pocket
and was afraid to talk. So in kind
of English/Swedish, I asked one
of the fellows standing there
if he knew where I could get work.
His name was David Anderson.
Ya, he said, *I heard you was a Swede.*

And David Anderson, he was a Swede too.

Later on, when Mr. Anderson
come back in for a load of hay—
all decent men had their own horses
those days and bought hay from the farmers—
he put me to work loading hay.

I made $25.00 a month.
It was all right,
I was young and always good help.

In Sweden you'd call me "Stayen,"
but over here they call me "Stone."

ABRAHAM TIESZIEN : DUTCH OVEN

Father would bring in a big armful of straw
or hay and I would feed the stove.
Mother would put her dough on the iron shelf
behind the doors and sit waiting
on the pine bench — a fork in her hands

ABRAHAM TIESZIEN : LOST

Silver Lake was about six miles away
and we had no water otherwise.
One day we went there by horse and wagon.
And after we got water, it was so dark
we couldn't find our way back. At home,
Dad was afraid of that so he split some boards
and started a fire on them and sent
my brother up to the top of the sod house
to hold a torch and bring us home.

MALTILDA DORMAN : AND THAT WAS THAT

Well, the government sent you. You filled
out a paper and they got you a job
teaching — then a friend talked about homesteading
and I said, *Fine, that's what I want to do* —
a woman can batch, you know!
Had 80 acres in Lyman County
to start with and when I got through with that
I filed on another one — I hired my house built,
just a cabin — tar-papered it myself,
alone on a windy day—
It just about had the best of me —
Then I decided I didn't like the place
and I wanted to move the cabin
to have a cave under it to keep things in
in the winter so I dug — I dug this cave
and I run into what we call pure shale
out here — and it was pretty rough —
the neighbor said, *What you need is a pick.*

Then I taught school in Sturgis
— on top a mountain one winter
winter, a couple winters,
and it was really hard climate —
I couldn't keep cattle 'cause I'd never know
where they were so I decided I'd keep sheep
— about as nice a work I ever got.

One day I rode a horse into Quinn
and it rained and rained all day,

kind of slop, slop, slop, and we shod
and we shod that horse — everything
was all right but I was wet — I needed
someone to lead me across that Cheyenne River—
I was afraid it would take the horse.
Anyway, someone rode up on a fine palomino
and I asked him, *Now would you go across*
that river and I'll follow you?
and he did and I did, and that was that.
On the second day the horse was going up
this slippery old road called "The Badlands Trail,"
— it was steep and I looked up and there were pine trees
all showing; then I saw something out of the northwest,
a great ball of fire as big as that stove there.
I watched the thing and it roared
and my horse stood straight up like that—
then I knew it had to be bad because I'm not crazy!
But I was on my way to Quinn that night
and I went on and the first place I came to
I said, *Could I stay the night?*
and that woman said, *No,*
we haven't any place to put anybody.
I said, *Yes, I can set up here*
in the kitchen. I said, *I'm willing to do anything—*
I was just too nervous to start for Quinn
when I didn't know where Quinn was anyway—
well, she fixed me up a place and kept me
and I got up the next morning and went to town for breakfast.

Later on I went to Yankton to get more
schooling — they consolidated my credits —

of course, I didn't have no high school
and I had to make that up, too —
somebody said I needed to earn more credits
and I told them, *Credits nothing!*
I've been teaching that stuff for years.

Franklin Fishback married Miss Mary Goodteacher.
—Moody County : October 5, 1873

JIM BURYANEK : MULES

I went to school about nine months
altogether in three years. Dad said,
Someone's got to lead the mule.
Someone's got to get in the hay.

CHURCH BELLS

They had a missionary that taught them how to make lace.
— Anonymous : YANKTON TRIBE

I used to love to hear the bells ring.
The Episcopal bell had a low voice.
The Presbyterian had a high voice.
You don't hear church bells anymore.

And I used to ask my grandmother,
What's the church bell mean?
What's it saying?
She'd say in Indian, *Wacekiye A u.*
Wacekiye A u.
Come to church. Come to church.

WALTER MILLER : WALLOWING

When I was a boy—
we went out to milk one evening
and here come a string of Indians—
40 or 50 wagons of them
and Mother didn't want to meet them
so we got a quilt or two and lay out here
in the wheat field. When Dad got home,
he bawled us out for wallowing on his wheat.
Oh, they never did hurt us any.

DICK SILER : WAS A NIGGER

Was a nigger down the road with two farms.
Had a team of horses, a team of mules,
but didn't own a harness. He'd let them
turn around and feed from the wagon.

One day a mule broke loose and he said,
Goddamn it, Trika, go anywhere you please.
It's all got to be plowed anyhow.

Nigger's name was Oscar Micheaux.
He moved to Chicago; wrote some books,
made a movie and got rich.

I bet he was crooked!

IV

THOMAS HUBBARD : BLIZZARD

George looked up and said, *Here comes a real blizzard.*
If we hurry up we can get to the S Ranch, I said.
So we took off his saddle — we used
them big Indian blankets for saddle blankets
them days and he cut a slice about that big,
square out of his blanket. Well, he cut two
of them out, one for me, one for him. Then he
took his knife, reached over and cut one of the strings
off his saddle in order to tie it around his head.
And he come over and he cut a string off my saddle.
I said, *Here, what the hell are you doing?*
He got to laughing — *You'll know what I'm a'doing*
before this is over. Now just keep moving.

I don't know whether I made 40 miles or not.
I was walking part near the most of the time,
leading my horse. Well, I came up on this hill
and I looked down in a little creek bed there,
quite a little timber on it, and I saw them three tepees.
Course, I made it down there. The old squaw
give me a bowl of soup. Jesus, that big!

It was sure good, and then she put me up
in the other tepee with a good hot fire.
And I slept there all the rest of the day and that night.
Now, George just followed up the creek
where he had a big contract for a bunch of horses.
The horses were being wintered there and these corrals
run clear across the creek and back and he thought
he'd be safe. He put his horse in the barn
and went to the house and built a roaring old fire
and stayed there till the next day, warm as could be.

I see a chief point North as he straddles
something. Something's in his left hand.
Down his back his headdress shivers in splendid color.
Ah! What! Yes, he carries the American flag.
His feathers are red, white and blue.
Anonymous : YANKTON SIOUX

SELMA ALVIDA BENSON : MARRIED

Mother had a disadvantaged love affair
in Norway and decided she wouldn't stay
— that's all. She came to America.
She traveled by train to her sister's home
in Brandt, S.D., but they let her off in Gary.

She didn't speak English. No one was around,
and all day she sat in the little old
lumber yard with her bundle. At night,
a man passed by with his wagon and took her
to the Norwegian family in town.
The next day she got a job at the Hort Hotel.

Well, every Sunday Mother'd visit this family—
it was here she met Dad and her friend
began to say: *You ought to marry this man.*
Mother said: *I'm so tired of working,
I don't even care if I do get married.*
But Dad said: *I don't even have a suit
to marry in.* And Mother said: *Well,
I'm working. I'll buy your suit.*
And that was $10.00. It was 1880
and they got married in this spot right here—
up by the railroad track.
Nothing but a grove of trees.

PETE LEMLEY : DEADWOOD

We was going to Deadwood. Me and him.
So, we started out and he didn't have any money.
We got up to the store and he bought a pair
of goddamned cheap shoes and by god, it got halfways
to Shendan, they played out — too damn little,
so I let him have my shoes and we headed
on to Deadwood. I had 75¢ left. Well,

we went out on the sidewalk picking our teeth
and didn't have a cent in the world
nor knew anybody and, by gosh, Frank Dean
came along with five spans of mules and a big load
of freight. He stopped and asked did we want jobs?
I clumb high up on the wagon and took a seat.
The other fellow set on the sacks behind.

And Frank Dean says, *Can you drive mules?*

I says, *I can drive all the mules I can
get ahead of me and I don't care how many.*

Have you ever broke any wild mules? he says.

I says, *I broke wild mules.*

He says, *We got a span that's whipped
these old skinners all out and we can't use them
and we can't catch them. I want them broke!*

I went out and found the mules down at a tent
about four miles below Hot Springs. Hell,
I had met with a horse trader
when I was about a kid, oh, 12 years old,
and helped him break horses.
I could rope and handle things.

Frank says, *I can give you $30.00 a month and board.*
Says, *How do you want to break them?*
I says, *All I need's a gentle mule
and a harness, a couple of halters and a rope.*

At about 9:00, he come by and I had this wild mule
caught and had him tied to this other mule
and they were walking around with the end
of the harness on. Bill and Victoria were their names,
ornery mules. I had old Victoria with her hindfoot
tied up and I was standing there playing
with her ears when Frank looked over the fence.

By God, boy, he says, *it kind of looks like you
got the best of them.*

Oh, I says, *Yes, I got them going
pretty good and I'm going to take Bill
out and work him this morning.*

Oh, God, he says, *don't take him out—
handle him in the corral,* he says.
He'll get away.

No, I says, *he won't.*

So I worked him that forenoon,
a couple, three, hours and played around
with them at the corral. By gosh, sir,
that night Frank calls me to come down to his tent.

Well, boy, he says, *you done what you said
you was going to last night. You told me
you could get them going good,* he says,
and if you can make a team out of them, he says,
I'll give you $50.00 a month.

And he did!

DICK SILER : KATYDID

I made $5.00 a day walking behind
a katydid — that's what they called
the breaking plow. It took four
horses to break the prairie to sod.

JEANETTE AGRANT : YOM KIPPUR

Mortgage payments were too high,
market prices too low. Money
was wasted on luxuries. Father drove
across the entire state for a sack of flour.
Cattle needed shelter and water,
but it cost too much to dig a well.
One year it was the Hessian fly.
The next year — the drought.
Then, on highest holy day, Yom Kippur,
the hay crops caught on fire.
We stayed until 1880,
long enough to buy the farm.

VIC BOWMAN : OFF TO SCHOOL

Some policemen come around to take me
to school. Mother pleaded and cried, but
the train come along the line bringing
Indians in from Rosebud and all over,

carloads of kids, me and the Hawk boys
and the Liver boys, crying like weaning calves,
trying to get away like wild ducks.
One boy just run. He got as far as Rapid.

Our hair was cut short; if we didn't understand
English they took a stick and rammed
it in our ears. You worked half a day
and went to school half a day.

If you talked you had to kneel and pray,
you had to stand at attention a number of hours,
you had to go to church each morning and pray.
They fed us slick beef; they sold the good,

then bought cheap meat. They sold the whole milk
then served us skim. The disciplinarian
sold the bigger boys booze. The matron of girls
had a mustache. She was half man and all bad.

Oh, everything bad happened there!

MRS. PEMBERTON AND MRS. DIETRICH : CALAMITY

"Well, Sir, we came to Spearfish
when I was a little girl.
We went to convent school there.
Sister was two years older."

"Our father was a doctor, you know.
He went as far as Mocroft to operate.
When Maury Tyler got his legs caught
in the threshing machine it was my father
went out there. He took off Maury Tyler's
legs on the kitchen table with nobody
to give the anesthetic."

"Yes, school was a lovely place to be
and if there was a stranger at the door,
why we kids would be peeking around the corner.
One day this very modest looking woman
came and she had on a long black skirt
and a black shawl around her shoulders
and a funny little hat. She brought
a little girl to board— a nice little thing
and timid as could be and so we played
with her — Calamity's little daughter.
I think her name was Jessie, Jessie Burke.
But anyway she was a nice little thing.
And one day we went to church and of course
the little girl, Calamity's daughter, had to go too,
and when we got up behind the schoolhouse,
why kids began throwing stones at us,

calling out, 'Calamity Jane,' 'Calamity Jane.'
And, well, they were just terrible kids,
boys hiding beside the schoolhouse and throwing stones
at us so when we came home the Sisters didn't
let the girl stay because of the notoriety.
And Calamity—why she didn't look anymore
like you'd picture Calamity Jane,
in pants and men's clothes!
She had a little old black skirt, I remember,
that dragged her tracks out. You'd never
think of her as a wild and wooly cowboy.
No. She had an old long draggy dress, and black.
I think she was quite a nice looking woman."

"No, I don't think she was. My father,
he was a doctor there, you know, Father said,
when she was young, she looked like an old woman.
Of course, Father practised medicine
in the horse and buggy days.
We had a regular old Englishman, Old Armstrong,
that used to take care of Father's teams.
Father went clear to Mocroft, wasn't it?
Or was it Sundance?

Well, anyway, Father amputated Maury Tyler's
legs out there on the kitchen table.
Father performed all kinds of surgery.
He was really quite a wonderful surgeon.
I think he took off Maury Tyler's legs.
It's a wonder he didn't bleed to death."

"Indeed!"

BUZZ GORHAM : BOGEDA BAR

The back bar and the front bar
of Dad's saloon come from the World's Fair.
They had craps, the wheel, 21,
Policy, and Fairbanks,
30 or 40 dealers.

There was none of them crooked.
Now they're all crooked.

Those ceiling fans turned around
slowly, just moving the air.
And if the lights went out,
you lit a candle and kept going.

Up there on the balcony
the girls sang and played.
They'd sing and play
and were very nice.
Course, I was just a kid.

MARTIN-HE-DOES-IT : CAIN & ABEL

Father, I'm going to ask you —
In the Bible, it says Adam and Eve,
everything all turned loose to them,
all kinds of fruit — then why they eat
the apple of the forbidden tree?
I don't believe it.
Must be something left out.

Then they got a son, Cain. Then Abel.
Cain murdered his brother Abel?
Then he run away?
And all the people say, *That's alright?*

Well, anyway, he run away, run away, run away,
and pretty soon God come in the cloud:

Where is brother Cain?

But Cain still run. Finally, he talks.
About a hundred years Cain come back,
visited his parents, oh, all kinds
of grandchildren and this and that.
And where the hell he get that woman,
I don't know.

I thought there was no other human being
in the world that time?
He must be married to some monkey

or something, I say. That's why the white people —
they come from the monkey!

Father, he say: *Martin, I'll tell you what
later on.* But he never did tell me.
He died. Yeah, there must be something there.
They say there was no other human.

Something's wrong, something
went in. There's got to be a punishment.
if something else is in it, I wanted him
to tell me. Priest, he was a priest,
and I only go to third grade.

*When we scratched the pox
off, our eyes went blind.*
                    —Anonymous : LAKOTA SIOUX

GUY GODDARD : PRAIRIE FIRE

That was the great thing in Sully County, 1889.

Smoke began to come right toward us
and the wind was blowing good.
Mother got so excited she didn't know
what to do. She took Ray in her arms,
and me by the hand, and started wandering.

Her voice trembled and she gave the words
of part of a song in the hymnal:
Oh, Jesus is a rock in a weary land,
And a shelter in the time of storm.

And you know her prayer must have been heard
because that fire, ravishing that it was,
did come. But it missed our place half a mile
or so and it didn't do a bit of damage.

MERT BUCKLEY : JINGLER

Well, they grazed 'em in the morning
off the bedground, and the last guard,
why they started 'em north and let 'em graze
—don't let 'em string out.
And the other fellows, the day men,
had breakfast by 4:00, then they come out
and relieved the last guard, don't you see?

The food was good enough—
beans and baking powder biscuits,
or sour dough, maybe, and bacon
and we'd have beef once in a while
if we could get to kill one. Lots of beans.
This old Blackbird could sure cook.
He used to bake 'em in a pot.
He'd have me drag up some right kind of wood
to make good coals and he'd bury
the beans in them black pots.
And a good lid on 'em and leave
them in the coals all night.
The next morning, they're nice and brown.

The cook'd have everything cleaned up
by about 5:00 and had put it on the mess wagon.
Then you had to take care of your rope corral,
put it on the bed wagon and then them fellows
string out these cattle after the wagon
and the horse wrangler goes ahead for the next camp.
Anybody else could get throwed off

and it didn't make much difference.
But sometimes there wouldn't be nobody
on the saddle horse but that jingler, don't you know.
He had to be on horseback all the time.
You couldn't corral no cattle on foot.

ELLA DELORIA : LEARNING ENGLISH

In our mission the minister read in Dakota,
then we had to put the stories into English.
Some of the words were so euphonious
they interested me right from the start.

One of the most beautiful was "riotous living,"
Another was "in the company of harlots." Harlots!
And then there was "famine" and all the rest.

EMMA HUETNER : ABOUT MY UNCLES

These two brothers decide they want to leave
South Dakota and go east to school.
They are young and they say:

Well, this is too hard. We won't get anywhere
farming for others. Let's go West first
and earn some money and then go East to school.

So they ride the rods to Bismarck where they work
in the harvest fields and when they get enough money
they build a boat. They are going to go
all the way back East on that boat,
you see, to go to college.

They build a little house on top the boat
but it's already November and there's ice
on the Missouri so bright it blinds them.
Oh, this ice and the ice chunks are out there
and they're in this little boat! Its rough.
And what happens is they come around a curve
and there's a branch of a tree sticking out
and that breaks their little house right off.

Well, they make it down the river a ways
and get as far as Ft. James, then Fred says:

I don't understand these people here.
What kind of language is that?

And they are Indians.
So, anyway they get out of there in the morning
and down the river they go again.
It gets worse and worse but they go
as far as Mobridge right up here on
the river, by this railroad bridge and they stop.

They need some food now because it's all
been knocked into the river when the house fell
so Fred walks to town and Oscar stays behind
to clean up. When Fred comes back he says:

This is an awful town. We've to get out.

And do you know they tried to go and couldn't.
They were frozen in. Stuck in Mobridge.
Each day they'd go back and forth to this little boat
until finally the man at the lumber yard said:

Why don't you stay?

But they wanted to go East!
Still, there was no getting out,
so they paid a dollar down
and put up a place for themselves
right where this house stands now!

CHARLES BARKLE : COLLEGE

I was 14, 15, working in the store
I was talking Norwegian
and I was talking Swedish
and I was talking Bohemian
and I was talking German —
that's what we had as customers
and I wanted to talk to them.

A school teacher named Dunning,
he comes in one day with one of those gallon
jugs. Playing with the language, I said,
"Hi, Mr. Dunning. You want some '*wine*gar?'"
"No," he said. "I want some '*gine*gar.'"
That's what put me in college. The words.

PETE LEMLEY : WORLD'S FAIR

Well, the cowboys, they went up and shot
into the Stronghold Table and got the Indians
after them, and led those Indians down
in this Little Corral Draw, staying just far
enough ahead of them, they could get them
any minute. And when they jammed the Indians
in this narrow place why these people
cut loose at them and shot them a bunch.
About 40, 50 Indians killed there.

But the Indians didn't chase 'em back.
They just came to carry away their dead
and wounded right after the fight.
The Indians are very careful about that.

Well, the cowboys got 8 pack horse loads
of Messiah shirts, saddles, and guns
off the Indians and they took them down
to the Chicago World's Fair there and charged
10¢ to see them. And that wasn't catsup
on those shirts either! No sir!

MR. AND MRS. BOWMAN

"It don't do your mind any good
to be pushed around like that."

"No — it makes a person bitter
or something. You can't look
at things straight anymore."

"There were people who helped
us in our lives but we'd put money
in the bank then the bank
would go broke."

"We ate an awful lot of beans,
stuff like that to keep alive.
We was broke when we got married ..."

"oh, we was always broke.
There's been a few good people
around and we appreciate it."

"We survived 18 years
by putting every penny
into land and cattle."

"You know they change the laws

all the time at Pine Ridge.
If an Indian gets out of place
the BIA gives reasons why
he can't lease the land."

"Gee, why do we have to fight
things like that?"

"We've had to fight all our lives.
As long as we drink the white man's
booze, spend his money and all that,
everything's peaceful."

"She says it
more better than I."

Alcohol spoiled the whole thing.
—Andrew DeRockbrain : TETON SIOUX

VINE DELORIA : WANTON APATHY

I can get along with the white man.
I can try to take part in American life
but I feel drained. I weep.
I have to go home, take off my collar.

My father taught me 33 old Indian songs.
I have a little thing I tap with.
I tap and I sing to get rejuvenated.

If I'm going to be enthusiastic,
If I'm going to have hope,
I've got to sing Indian.

JIM BURYANEK : I'LL SAY ONE THING

I've enjoyed living out here.
I had two of the finer boys
anyone ever had. I got one left.

I've seen good times and some hard times —
grasshoppers, the droughts, duststorms.
We always got by someway.

I had two of the finer hounds anyone
ever had — stag hounds. If I didn't take
them out, they'd go by themselves.

101

GALE SMALL : TEA PARTY

Dad was in his dugout and he saw
a man across the river walking.
Dad was walking too, just looking
because that's all he had to do.
He went over to the river and hailed
him and the man took off his clothes
and swam across. In the dugout
they had supper and a real nice visit.

And when they got through, this man,
Mr. Briggs, stripped and swam across again,
then he put on his clothes and went
down the road to file on some land.

ALFRED ZIEGLER : TRIBAL LAND

As long as the grass grows,
As long as the river flows,
As long as you are dead and buried.
This will be your land.
— from The Laramie Treaty, 1868

Oh, it's a complicated thing, I don't know.
If you sit down and think of it, you get confused.
I tell you, I'll never understand. They say
we're pretty well off, the land's allotted,
each owns so much. But I don't own nothing.
If I die my land goes up in smoke. It's like owning
that sky. You give me that sky; I look at it
and say I own it, but I can't eat it or touch it.

MR. EVANS : A WELCOME CUP

My grandmother sat on a little board
in front of the prairie schooner holding
the baby, Stanley, and drove the horses.
Grandfather helped the boys drive the cattle alongside.
The little calves played out easily.

After weeks of wearisome travel, the family
reached the Missouri River and from there
went on to Hayes where Grandmother received
a warm cup of coffee from Mr. William Hopkins.
A very welcome cup, she said.

They were like pilgrims —
they had to make everything they ate,
or wore, or used. Most meat was preserved.
All the family gathered buffalo berries,
wild plums, wild cherries and currants.
These Grandmother canned without sugar
for the long winter months.

Soon, Grandfather constructed an ice house
not far from the cellar and that summer
the boys dug a hole there with the post auger
and discovered water. At first, everyone
was quite excited about pure, cool,

spring water in the cellar
but it proved to be melted ice seeping through.

At that time each section of the state
tried to secure the most settlers
and Grandmother was especially interested
in locating the capitol in Pierre.
Since the Evans family was the first family
between Phillip and Ft. Pierre,
nearly all prospective settlers gave them a visit.

Each summer each settler started to complain
about the water situation. So immediately,
Grandmother would guide them to the cellar
and give them a drink of crystal water from the well.
Everyone marveled at the taste and thought it a spring.
Grandmother would feed them, then show her rich
garden where she once raised a pumpkin
weighing 75 pounds and a cucumber 22 inches long.
These she displayed, hoping to influence settlers to stay.
And they did.

V

Don't you see the Whites
on the reservation are afraid
of you? Why do you pray to Great Wakan Tanka
to send the Savior to earth?
The remedy lies in your hands. Be men,
not children. You have a perfect right to dance!
    —from *The Illustrated American* (January 17, 1891)

GHOST DANCE

I will try to make a song here.
— Hunkpapa drummer

And they all join hands and they sing in a kind of slow way
And they use their hands back and forth, the one man here
And the lady there and they divide and stand in a circle
And the drummer is in the center and they start singing
And they beat the drum and they start dancing and keep on dancing
And the dancing goes on all through the night till daybreak

And they say they see the spirits of the dead ones
Or they say they see their relatives
They say they hear the coming of the Messiah

And they danced at Wounded Knee and the soldiers tried to stop them
And they surrendered to the army and laid down their arms but one
And he shot an officer and the great massacre happened
And they killed over 200 persons menfolk women
And children and it was winter and they were scattered all over
And frozen Chief Big Foot was one of them And Short Bull was one
He said *We have the ghost shirts on and they are bulletproof.*

PRAYER OF THE GHOST DANCE PRIEST

Now, Grandfather God,
we remember what you told
us and give thanks.

One day I was sick
and I turned to you and you
granted me good health.

I fulfilled all my promises
and now I live in peace among my people,
wind-blown, but happy.

SITTING BULL

Sitting Bull was chief
and he didn't want his people to move.
He didn't want his people to move.
And that's why they killed him.
He didn't want his people to move.

*I have seen all those people come—
all the Long Knives. They are thick
as flies. You are going to have to live
with them. You are going to have to learn
what they do and do it well!*
—Spotted Tail

ROBERT NORMAN : WOUNDED KNEE

I saw Red Cloud try to stop them building the railroad.
He knew the danger and tried to stop it but he was not
quite big enough. He did the best he could— ruined a lot
of rail for them. He was fighting for his people, but it
was just one of those things that open the country and
that. Times change.

On Christmas day we started South—
I'll never forget that breakfast—
hardtack and frozen sowbelly.
We tramped all Christmas day until dark.
When we got to our camp grounds we took our shovels
and shoveled snow in order to pitch our Sibley tents,
round ones with the hot stoves in them.
It was pretty close to that Creek of Wounded Knee.
The order was given to a bunch to disarm the Indians
somewhere around the morning of the 29th.
They pointed out a squad to go in and take away
their rifles and ammunition.
Well, of course, all the bucks had blankets
around them and had those little guns,
so the Lieutenant in charge of the disarming squad,
he got kinda suspicious, and said:
You got other arms, don't you?
No, that's all we got, they said.
Rip those goldarn blankets off them, boys, he said.
Let's see what they got.

And there they were—brand new Springfields and some other;
I forget. They had all kinds of them.
Anyhow, they were properly ferreted out, you know.
Had vests around their shoulders with ammunition

and that's what made the trouble.
The officers wouldn't stand for it.

There was an old squaw come up around the —
I forget the Lieutenant's name —
and she had an old tomahawk there
and she hit that Lieutenant right in his head
and that's when it started — the trouble.

We were ordered to make a squirmish —
they called it a "squirmish" — line
around those Indians standing there.
Then Colonel Sumner told them
to give up or else they'd be sorry.
Now, they wouldn't give up their guns.
They'd fight before do that; that's all there is to it!

Now, you see, we'd be laying outside
all these nights, you know, and frozen
and pretty well sick of it so the Colonel says,
Now, boys, he says, *We're going to shoot
a couple volleys right over their heads.
We want to go home.*
But they went around the squirmish line and said,
*Who in heck is going to shoot over their heads.
We want to go home.*
So, they went around the line and said,

Shoot 'em down. Shoot 'em down.
Let's get through with it.

It lasted maybe half an hour,
maybe three quarters.
We had one Hotchkisser with us.
Kind of a cannon. It was over very quickly
when quite a number of soldiers were killed —
30 I think it was killed,
and 30 that were wounded.
This was late in the afternoon.
It was getting dark, and the boys,
they were getting pretty sick and tired of it,
so Sumner says, *Let them lay there.*
We'll go out and pick them up in the morning.
So in the morning, they ordered out the mule team
to pick them up; there'd been a storm that night
and the bodies were frozen.
They piled them up in the wagon just like cordwood.
One was identified as Yellow Bird.
I sure remember him laying on top of his tepee.
Then they brought them up to this trench and buried them.

I never have been back there since it happened.
I should have gone back there and homesteaded.
Had some darn nice land there, as you know.

MERT BUCKLEY : FORT YATES

The roads is all washed out.

Oh, gosh, there ain't nothing there anymore,
just a little bit of the old agency.
There's no part of Fort Yates, the soldier part,
left. And do you know, I met 7 old fellows around there
and they don't know a cockeyed thing
about the stuff that happened in them days.

By golly, they don't remember it or care.
I just got one fellow, Charlie LeBeau,
and had a good visit with him.
He's the only one what struck.
He remembered the McLaughlin boys. Mary,
my sister, used to work for Major McLaughlin,
and we kids would go over there to play.

It would be nice if I could find
somebody there at Winona and cross the river
and see them again. I would like to go
back to the old flat on the big Mo.,
the homestead, even if it's not there.

BILLY POWELL'S SMILE

Coming home from Oregon
on the sleeper past Pennington
I looked out at early morning
and saw a rider galloping.

I told my wife: *Quick! Look out
the window before we pass him.*

She looked out the window
then she looked at me:
*That's the best smile
you've had since you left South Dakota.*

And I've still got that smile
for South Dakota.

W. H. STODDARD : HURLEY CEMETERY

We ask ourselves: *Who sleeps here?*
Is this his mark made by the plow on the prairie?

And here is a small mound sodded over with green.
We ask: *Who is buried here?*
Some baby whose mother moved far away?

Drop a rose in their memory.

And here is the resting place
of an unnamed soldier from the Civil War.

Shall we let the sunflowers and thistles
gnaw around the mounds?
The bramble and the brush?

HAROLD LEE : COUNTING BACK

1869 Grandfather emigrated from Norway
1872 homesteaded
1875 he was born
1896 Father married
1897 I was born
1915 35 bushels an acre was a good crop
1928 I married
     4 daughters born
1930 depression and dust storms
1931 oats 7¢ a bushel, corn 12¢, eggs 5¢ a dozen
     .65 a bushel was high
1939 went into the dairy business
     203 people lived in Brandon
1940 1st milking parlor and pipeline milkers with
     2 zero vacuum bulk tanks installed
     102 Holsteins milked
1944 I organized Sioux Valley Milk Producers Assoc.
     15 years their president
1960 1,500 people lived in Brandon
     Served 7 years on the school board,
     2 terms on the legislature
1961, retired!

WALTER LaCAINE : THE HEYOKA

Ho! Hello!
Rid of me want you?
Back to take it away again come you?

Why? say I

Away my life take you
Away my buffalo take you
Away all my Indian take you

Now, soon as I got enjoying myself,
Around come you, around sneak you, around work you
Away that Indian again take you.

> *Whoever made those stories — they fooled up this history, you know. They fool people.*
>
> —Dick Fools Bull : ROSEBUD SIOUX

HISTORICAL EVENTS : DAKOTA TERRITORY, 1743-1890

1743	François and Louis-Verendrye, French explorers, reached central South Dakota.
1760	Oglala and Brule Sioux reached the Missouri River.
1775-76	Oglala war party discovered the Black Hills.
1804	Lewis and Clark met delegation of Yankton Sioux at Missouri River Camp.
1832	Pierre Chouteau built a fur post on the west bank of the Missouri River which later became Ft. Pierre.
1851	July, Santee Sioux ceded to the Federal Government all lands east of the Big Sioux River except for a ten mile stretch of reservation land.
1854	Area became Nebraska Territory.
1858	April 19, the Yankton Tribe ceded to the U.S. 400,000 acres in eastern and central South Dakota.
1861	478 settlers representing the entire population of Dakota (and then some) signed a petition for territorial government, granted on March 2 by President Buchanan who detached from Nebraska Territory that portion lying north of the 43rd parallel, thus placing the entire Upper Missouri Valley under a single jurisdiction.
1862	Santee Sioux uprising at the upper Minnesota agency and across adjacent territories resulted in the deaths of 700 white settlers and 100 soldiers.
1864	Some far western area is lost to Montana and Wyoming.
1868	The Laramie Treaty set apart land, including the Black Hills, as The Great Sioux Reservation.

1870	Dakota Territory increased in population to 10,000. The majority of settlers came from nearby states; foreign born immigrants came largely from Scandinavia, Germany, Russia, and Bohemia.
1873	Dakota Southern Railroad line was established between Sioux City, IA, and Yankton, S.D., which served as an outfitting point for the Black Hills.
1874	Gold is discovered in the Black Hills.
1876	June 25, General George Custer and 200 men of the Seventh Cavalry were killed fighting Sioux and Cheyenne Indians at The Battle of the Little Bighorn.
1877	Sioux Indians relinquished land in the Black Hills to the United States.
1878	100,000 head of cattle ranged in the Black Hills.
1878-87	Homesteaders filed on 24,000,000 acres of land.
1886	July 4, first railroad train to Rapid City.
1887	Prairie fires, blizzards, and unfair labor practices created an agricultural depression.
1889	November 2, South Dakota becomes a state with its capitol in Pierre.
1890	December 29, U.S. Cavalry troops killed approximately 200 Lakota Sioux men, women and children at Wounded Knee.
	328,559 settlers lived in South Dakota.

APPENDIX : GUIDE TO THE SOUTH DAKOTA ORAL HISTORY AND AMERICAN INDIAN PROJECT TAPES : UNIVERSITY OF SOUTH DAKOTA

NAMES	TAPE NUMBER	
Agrant, Jeanette L.	1108	
Albrecht, Julius J.	44	
Anderson, Marie	1278	
Ashley, Rachael	360	AIP
Badlands (anon.)	18	
Barkie, Charles	200	
Before Looms (anon.)	92	AIP
Begeman, Anna	967	
Benson, Selma	383	
Bowman, Vic	1105	AIP
Buckley, Mert	91	
Bucholz, Dave	845	
Burnett, James	148	AIP
Buryanek, Jim	829	
Church Bells (anon.)	92	AIP
Cummins, John	635	AIP
Deloria, Ella	386	AIP
Deloria, Vine	82	AIP
Dorman, Maltilda	26	
Eastman, Mae	754	AIP
1834: Missionaries (anon.)	438	AIP
Eller, Cornelia	773	AIP
Mr. Evans	133	
Fools Bull, Dick	741	AIP
Ghost Dance (anon.)	125	AIP
Goddard, Guy	174	
Gorham, Buzz	464	
Gushurst, Albert	656	
Haxby, Orpha	102	
He-Does-It, Martin	463	AIP
Heidepriem, Eric	324	
Heminger, Phillip	158	AIP
Hubbard, Thomas	157	
Huetner, Emma	304	
Johnson, Mrs. River	1106	AIP
Keeble, Jonas	437	AIP
Kills-in-Sight, George	25	AIP
LaCaine, Walter	72	AIP

Lee, Harold	1084	
Lemley, Pete	542	
Littleton, Paul	742	AIP
Martin-He-Does-It	463	AIP
Miller, Walter	322	
Norman, Robert	95	
Old Coyote, Barney	596	AIP
Pearsall, Fred	774	AIP
Pemberton, Mrs. and Dietrich, Mrs.	92	
Picotte, Paul	428	AIP
Powell, Billy	133	
Red Owl, Fra	664	AIP
Schenck, Edna	219	
Siler, Dick	871	
Sitting Bull (anon.)	438	AIP
Small, Gale	208	
Stepina, Gale (daughter of Joseph)	824	
Stoddard, W.H.	1278	
Stone, Knute	898	
Stops, Roger	641	AIP
Swan, Lucy	691	AIP
Tieszen, Abraham	50	
Whalen, Jesse	20	
Woman Who Waddles (Cheyenne anon.)	428	AIP
Ziegler, Alfred	785	AIP

EXPLANATION OF NOTATIONS:
AIP : *American Indian Project* (part of total *Oral History Collection, University of South Dakota.*)

SELECTED BIBLIOGRAPHY

Anon. "Ghost Dance," *The Illustrated American*. 17 Jan., 1891, pp. 328-335.

Anon. *Yankton Daily Press and Dakotan*, 5 June, 1875, p. 3.

Bear, Standing. *My People The Sioux*. Univ. of Nebraska, Lincoln, 1975.

Connell, Evan. *Son of the Morning Star*. Albany, CA: North Point Press, 1984.

Hanson, James Austin. *Metal Weapons, Tools and Ornaments of the Teton Dakota Indians*. Univ. of Nebraska, Lincoln, 1975.

Hassrick, Royal B. *The Sioux*. Univ. of Oklahoma, 1964.

Hyde, George E. *Red Cloud's Folk: A History of the Oglala Sioux Indians*. Univ. of Oklahoma, Norman, 1937.

———. *A Sioux Chronicle*. Univ. of Oklahoma, Norman, 1961.

Jaffe, Dan. *Dan Freeman*. Univ. of Nebraska, Lincoln, 1967.

Olson, Callie Ann. "One Woman's Story," *South Dakota Magazine*. March, 1986, pp. 37-39.

Original Journals of Lewis and Clark. Introduction by Bernard De Voto. New York: Arno Press, 1969.

Schell, Herbert S. *History of South Dakota*. Univ. of Nebraska, Lincoln, 1961.

South Dakota Oral History Project. South Dakota, Pierre/Vermillion.

Stratton, Joan. *Pioneer Women*. New York: Simon and Schuster, 1981.

Terrell, John Upton. *Sioux Trails*. New York: McGraw-Hill, 1974.

To Be An Indian. Ed. Joseph H. Cash and Herbert T. Hoover. Holt, Rinehart, and Winston, 1971.

Walker, James R. *Lakota Belief and Ritual*. Univ. of Nebraska, Lincoln, 1980.

SYLVIA GRIFFITH WHEELER's book of poems, *Dancing Alone*, was published by BkMk Press in 1991. Her other books include *City Limits*, poems; *In the Middle: Midwestern Women Poets*, anthology; and *For Kids, By Kids*, anthology. Her play, *This Fool History*, based on South Dakota Oral History Tapes, began touring in 1990 and won the Fargo-Moorehead Community Theatre Midwestern Playwright's Merit Award in 1988. Sylvia Wheeler's poetry has often been anthologized. She has won numerous awards including the Gwendolyn Brooks Poetry Prize from the Society for the Study of Midwestern Literature, a Kansas Arts Council Award for Fiction, and a South Dakota Arts Council Individual Artist Award. Currently she is an Associate Professor of English at the University of South Dakota.

JAMES COOK

James Cook is a Denver-based photojournalist whose work has appeared in *Time, Newsweek* and other magazines for more than a decade. Commencing from his first trip to Wounded Knee, South Dakota in 1984, his work includes a series of personal projects regarding Native Americans. His documentation of Wounded Knee received national attention when it was included in "Ten Thousand Eyes," a PBS-Television broadcast about photography. Currently, Cook is working on his most ambitious project: photographing dancers and landscapes representing tribes from all regions of the country in their native terrain.

CONGER BEASLEY, JR.

Conger Beasley, Jr. was born in St. Joseph, Missouri, and educated in Connecticut and New York City. He is the author of two novels, two volumes of short fiction, and two books of poetry. A volume of essays, *Sun Dancers and River Demons* (University of Arkansas Press, 1990), won the Thorpe Menn Award for Literary Excellence. Beasley writes regularly for the environmental journals *E* and *Buzzworm*, and has done interpretive work for the National Park Service. He lives in Kansas City, Missouri.

Dancing Alone, poetry by Sylvia Griffith Wheeler. This is tough stuff, full of stubble and without complaint; a poetry that will not look away. ... There is no posing here, no literary flourishes—only real tracks of life across the landscape.
$7.50, 68 pages, paper.

The Darmstadt Orchids, poetry by Stuart Friebert. Poems with deep and diverse roots in Middle Europe. They give us a sense of tangled origins and tumultuous feelings.
$9.25, 64 pages, cloth with jacket

Sleepwalking Beneath the Stars, poetry by Howard Schwartz. "Schwartz shows a remarkable skill in reaching readers of many levels of experience, and of many ages and faiths ... these "Sleepwalking" pieces seem ethereal, meditative and observant." —*Judith Baumel*.
$9.50, 64 pages, cloth with jacket

Night Vision, poetry by Neal Bowers. "He writes as the jazzman improvises. ... Bowers' poems rise from his gut; they have the feel of experience. The result is an authentic collection that lingers in the mind." —*Michael Bugeja*.
$9.25, 68 pages, cloth with jacket

Someday Songs, poetry by Rochelle Ratner, with illustrations by Bernard Solomon. "Profound and beautiful poems. ... There is much tenderness here and much joy. These poems nourish. Parallels with Akhmatova are to the point." —*Robert Peters*.
$9.50, 68 pages, cloth with jacket

Hanging Out with the Crows, poetry by David Allan Evans. Evans has been an excellent poet for years, and here he is at his best.... These are tough-minded and graceful poems. The reader keeps on saying, "Yes. Right. This is the real thing." —*James Whitehead*.
$9.25, 64 pages, cloth with jacket

The Curandero, stories by Daniel Curley. Curley's sense of irony is great; his sense of language and form, subtle and precise. These stories take those special readers who want special writers into the imaginations and fears and thwarted dreams of people who have wandered into the depths.
$12.95, 136 pages, cloth with jacket.

Jerusalem As She Is, poetry by Shlomo Vinner; trans. by Laya Firestone-Seghi, Seymour Mayne and Howard Schwartz. Remarkable even in translation, these poems provide a sense of power of the original Hebrew. Winner of the Acum Prize and the Jerusalem Literary Foundation Prize, Vinner demonstrates the ambiguities of life in Israel between the ancient and the modern.
$8.95, 96 pages, paper.

Urbane Tales, short stories by Raymond Johnson. The intelligence, compassion, elegance, and sense of mortality within these stories infiltrate the reader's consciousness. Carefully wrought and sophisticated, *Urbane Tales* should satisfy those who demand grace without sacrificing the grip of reality.
$12.95, 96 pages, cloth with jacket.

A Story To Tell, poetry by Michael Paul Novak. Soundly made poems by a man firmly in the world who looks beyond surfaces and certainties. "Remarkable immediacy ... Novak brings a reader as close to the moment of experience as is possible with uncomplicated, graceful language, palpable feeling." —*Kansas City Star*.
$9.50, 72 pages, cloth with jacket